Festivals

My Hanukkah

Monica Hughes

Heinemann
LIBRARY

www.heinemann.co.uk/library

Visit our website to find out more information about **Heinemann Library** books.

To order:
- ☎ Phone 44 (0) 1865 888066
- 🖹 Send a fax to 44 (0) 1865 314091
- 💻 Visit the Heinemann Bookshop at www.heinemann.co.uk/library to browse our catalogue and order online.

First published in Great Britain by Heinemann Library, Halley Court, Jordan Hill, Oxford OX2 8EJ, part of Harcourt Education.
Heinemann is a registered trademark of Harcourt Education Ltd.

Editorial: Sarah Eason and Georga Godwin
Design: Jo Hinton-Malivoire and Tokay, Bicester, UK (www.tokay.co.uk)
Picture Research: Rosie Garai
Production: Séverine Ribierre

Originated by Dot Gradations Ltd
Printed and bound in China by South China Printing Company

10 digit ISBN 0 431 18631 6 (hardback)
13 digit ISBN 978 0 431 18631 3 (hardback)
07 06 05 04 03
10 9 8 7 6 5 4 3 2 1

10 digit ISBN 0 431 18637 5 (paperback)
13 digit ISBN 978 0 431 18637 5 (paperback)
08
10 9 8 7 6 5 4

British Library Cataloguing in Publication Data
Hughes, Monica
Little Nippers Festivals Hanukkah
296.4'35
A full catalogue record for this book is available from the British Library.

Acknowledgements
The Publishers would like to thank Chris Schwarz and Getty Images\Alex Wong p. **19** and Getty Images\Larry Eatz p. **12** for permission to reproduce photographs.

Cover photograph of the family meal, reproduced with permission of Chris Schwarz.

The Publishers would like to thank the Ryde family and Philip Emmett for their assistance in the preparation of this book.

Every effort has been made to contact copyright holders of any material reproduced in this book. Any omissions will be rectified in subsequent printings if notice is given to the Publishers.

Contents

At school

It's **fun** getting ready for Hanukkah at school.

We all love listening to
the Hanukkah story.

In the kitchen

Mmmm!

My Mum makes delicious apple sauce.

6

I can't wait to taste the doughnuts.

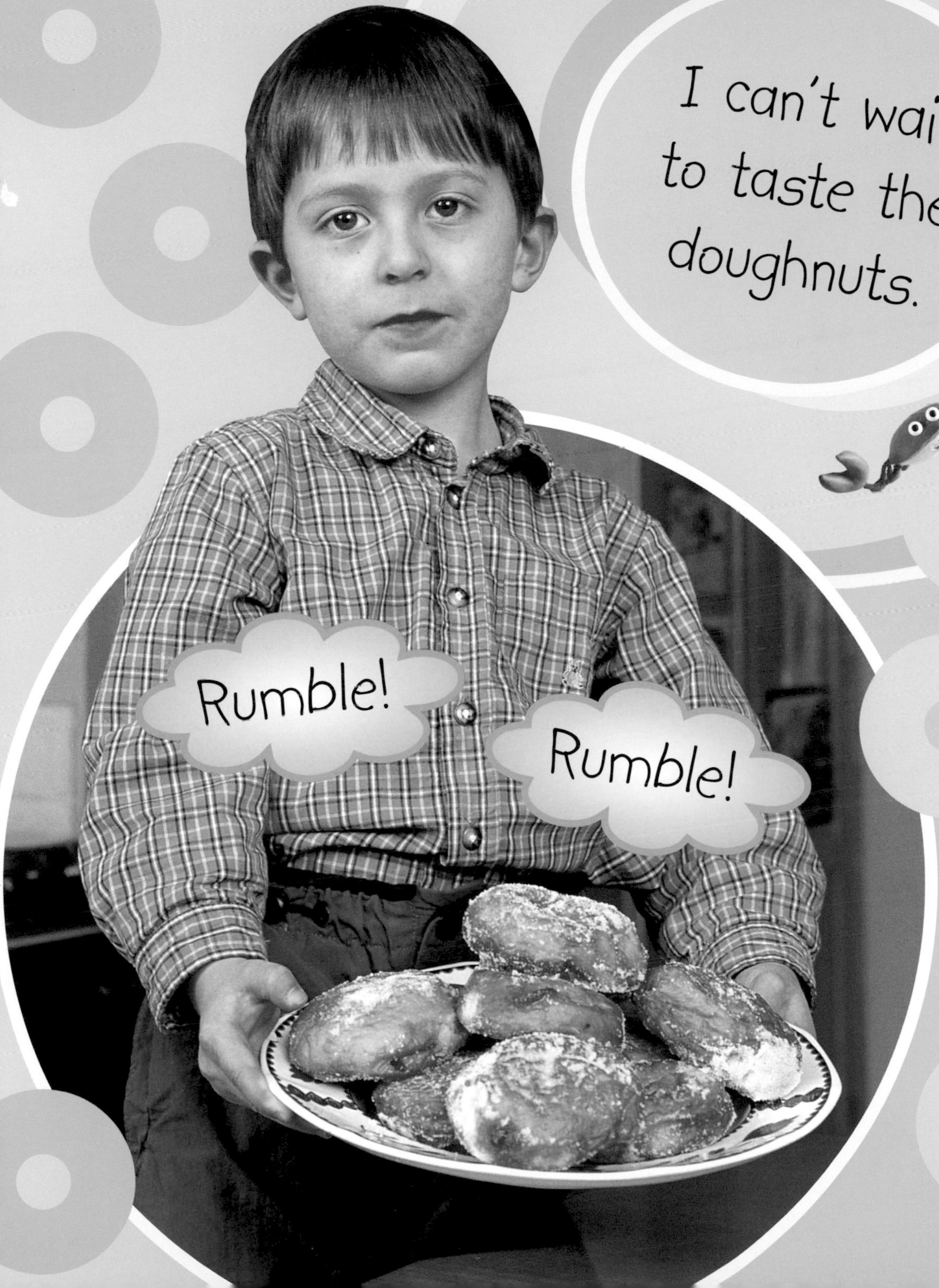

Cooking latkes

I like helping to make potato
pancakes for Hanukkah.

Yum!

Yum!

Don't the latkes look delicious!

The hanukiah

I hope we have enough candles for the eight nights of Hanukkah.

1, 2, 3, 4...

Tonight we'll light
candles on the hanukiah
for the third night.

I love the way the candles flicker on our little hanukiah.

Some hanukiot
are much bigger
than ours!

Presents

What will there be inside my first Hanukkah present?

It's the eighth night of Hanukkah and time for the last present.

More presents

Mum and Dad only had Hanukkah chocolate money when they were little.

But they like their Hanukkah presents today!

Thank you!

17

A family meal

I know all the words
when we sing Mao Tzur.

Now it's time to enjoy our meal together.

Spinning the dreidel

I hope I don't get 'nun'!

My grandpa is very good at playing dreidel.

Ready for a party

Don't we look **smart?**

It's always good fun at a Hanukkah party. **Happy Hanukkah!**

Index

The end

Notes for adults

Most festivals and celebrations share common elements that will be familiar to the young child, such as new clothes, special food, sending and receiving cards and presents, giving to charity, being with family and friends and a busy and exciting build-up time. It is important that the child has an opportunity to compare and contrast their own experiences with those of the children in the book. This will be helped by asking the child open-ended questions, using phrases like: What do you remember about …? What did we do …? Where did we go …? Who did we see …? How did you feel …?

Hanukkah is a Jewish celebration of light rather than a religious festival. It is centred in the home and is a special time for children. It takes place in November or December and lasts for eight days. A special hanukiah (candle stick) is used with two candles burnt (one being a 'servant' candle) on the first night and an additional candle lit from the 'servant' candle each night during the celebration.

Follow up activities could include making a Hanukkah card for a Jewish friend, finding a recipe for latkes (potato cakes), playing the dreidel game and working out how many candles are needed when new candles (plus the 'servant' candle) are used each day.